BAD DAY
ICE CREAM

Published by Familius LLC, www.familius.com

Familius books are available at special discounts for bulk purchases, whether for sales
promotions or for family or corporate use. For more information, contact Familius Sales
at 559 876 2170 or email orders@familius.com.

Library of Congress Cataloging-in-Publication Data
2019932216

Print ISBN 9781641701372
Ebook ISBN 9781641702010

Printed in China

Edited by Katharine Hale, Peg Sandkam, and Alison Strobel
Cover design by David Miles
Book design by Brooke Jorden
Photography sourced from Shutterstock.com
Special thanks to Julie Gransee from *Lovely Little Kitchen* and
Neha Chouhan from *Four-Eyed Cook* for use of their photography.

10 9 8 7 6 5 4 3 2 1

First Edition

KATHRYN
THOMPSON

RECIPES BY
BARBARA
BEERY

BAD DAY ICE CREAM

50 RECIPES THAT MAKE EVERYTHING BETTER

To our friend suffering through a big, fat, stinky, no-good, awful, cry-it-out, fist-pounding, bummer of a day.

Yeah. We're talking to you.

DISCLAIMER

You may be a good candidate for ice cream if you enjoy deliciousness and are capable of ingesting food. Ask your doctor if ice cream is right for you. If you are new to ice cream making, have trouble consuming mouthwatering foods, or feel dizzy at the sight of delectable confections, please contact your health care provider. Kathryn and Barbara are not medically licensed to treat bad days and serve in a dessert advisory capacity only.

CONTENTS

INTRODUCTION

*B*ad days are the worst. They're called "bad" for a reason. Whether your goldfish just went to the big glass bowl in the sky or you smashed your car before even making the first payment, you know a bad day when you see it.

And bad days require support. They require "treat"ment. We want to help you discover exactly what kind of treat will best mitigate the negative effects of your personal bummer day.

We're not advocating drowning your sorrows or binging on food so you don't have to deal with your problems. Spoiler alert—you always have to deal with your problems. Think of this book as a list of "whine pairings"—just the right spoonful of sugar to help the yucky medicine of your bad day go down and, hopefully, stay down.

Obviously, you may need to put some planning into this. When you're frazzled and burnt out, you may not have the energy to craft the perfect culinary prescription. Think ahead. If you know tomorrow could bring an avalanche of science fair homework, whip up a batch of Nerds Nightmare Ice Cream just in case.

You can also employ minions to help. If you're fighting the flu, maybe a kind roommate or teenage son can throw together some Gloop 2.0 and spoon-feed you.

Whatever you do, take care of business one tiny step at a time. And remember, you've got this. No bad day can last forever.

—Barbara and Kathryn

ABOUT US

BARBARA BEERY is a bestselling cookbook author and facetiously lauded confectionery apothecary.

KATHRYN THOMPSON is a self-certified, imminently renowned ice cream clinician, with years of experience consuming and prescribing frozen desserts.

BARBARA'S ICE CREAM HACKS

*I*ce cream. We love it. We want it. We need it. We eat it. Here are some tips and tricks to get the most out of your ice cream–making experience.

CHILL OUT: EQUIPMENT

- While some of the recipes in this book require an ice cream maker, many do not! That said, if a recipe includes this symbol 🪣, we do recommend using an electric ice cream maker.

- All of the process times for ice creams made with an electric ice cream maker are based on the Cuisinart ICE-21 1.5 Quart Frozen Yogurt, Ice Cream and Sorbet Maker, a popular model and the one I use.

- Ice cream made in an ice cream maker can be eaten immediately after processing for a soft serve texture. If you desire a harder ice cream texture, freeze for a couple hours before serving.

- The base of an electric ice cream maker must be chilled in the freezer for at least twenty-four hours before use. If not completely chilled, it will never make ice cream. If you have room in your freezer, just keep it there. Be ready for any ice cream emergency!

- A cooked ice cream base must be completely chilled before processing in an ice cream maker. If used immediately, it will never freeze to a firm consistency. If you have time, make a cooked ice cream base the day before you need the ice cream. It's safe to leave in your refrigerator up to three days before processing.

- In a hurry? Look for recipes with the Q&E symbol—these require little to no freeze time and a quick and easy prep! Ready within an hour.

- Recipes in this cookbook usually make between one and one and one half quarts. Most standard ice cream makers are equipped with a one and one half–quart base. Check your ice cream maker to be sure.

- Servings per recipe may vary according to your actual serving size.

- Homemade ice creams contain less air than purchased ice creams and will solidify rock hard in the freezer. Remember to remove your homemade ice cream from the freezer about ten minutes prior to serving to make it scoopable.

- For a frosty (and very professional) presentation, chill cups, glasses, or bowls in the freezer for two to three hours before serving.

THE RiGHT STUFF: iCE CREAM iNGREDiENTS

- **SUGAR:** For uncooked ice creams, use superfine sugar instead of regular granulated sugar. Why? Superfine sugar dissolves completely when ingredients are not heated or cooked. No superfine sugar in the house? Throw regular granulated sugar into a blender or food processor and whirl around for a minute. Voilà—superfine sugar!

- **HONEY, AGAVE, AND MAPLE SYRUP:** Use whichever you have in the house. Honey has a higher sugar content and is a bit sweeter than the other two.

- **WHIPPED CREAM:** So many options—homemade, canned, or frozen whipped topping. Which one is best? It's really up to you. Personally, I find homemade whipped cream always tastes best, but a little squirt from a can is better for presentation on a parfait. Unless specified, use the whipped cream of your choice.

- **SALT:** Don't omit it! A pinch of salt (less than one-quarter teaspoon) makes the sweet taste sweeter. Really.

- **VANILLA:** Ahh, vanilla. It's what makes ice cream, cakes, and cookies taste their best. When a recipe in this book calls for vanilla, you can use either **vanilla extract** or **vanilla bean paste**. What's the difference? Vanilla bean paste is scraped out of the inside of a vanilla bean. While more expensive, it has a more intense flavor and also adds the specks of vanilla you see in high-quality ice cream. If you choose to use extract instead, use the best you can afford. *Never* use imitation vanilla—or any imitation extract, for that matter. Please. Whatever you choose, there's no need to convert—measure for measure, paste and extract can be used interchangeably.

CHAPTER ONE

MiLD IRRiTATiON

While some bad days are soul crushing, others are just annoying. If you're suffering from mild irritation, please look to the remedies in this chapter. Whether you're having a bad hair day, your favorite house plant just died, or you battled traffic for two hours getting home from work, we've got you covered.

These lighthearted, delicious treats will taste amazing as you relax away your frustration after an irritating day.

CRAZY FUNFETTI ICE CREAM CAKE JARS

*I*f your name isn't Rapunzel or Samson, you probably get your hair cut every once in a while. There are good stylists, and there are terrible stylists. Sometimes a great stylist just has an off day.

Sometimes you ask your sister to give you layers like Rachel from *Friends*, but you end up looking more like David Bowie in *Labyrinth*. And you cry. Because no seventeen-year-old girl growing up in the nineties wants to look like a goblin king. Hypothetically speaking.

Ahem.

And it's not just bad cuts. You can have a great cut and still end up looking cuckoo-nuts some mornings. How is it that hair is composed entirely of dead cells but somehow still has a mind of its own?

Sometimes you can't control your hair, and that's no fun. But you *can* control exactly how many layers of deliciousness go into these Crazy Funfetti Ice Cream Cake Jars. Savor them slowly over the next few weeks, like it's your job. Meanwhile, your hair will do *its* job— grow and get back to normal!

Prep time for cake: 30-40 minutes
Prep time to assemble: 5 minutes
Makes 4-5 half-pint jars

INGREDIENTS

1 box Funfetti cake mix

1 pint ice cream or sorbet, any flavor

Rainbow sprinkles, to garnish

4-5 Mason jars (4 ounces each)

DIRECTIONS

① Prepare cake mix according to directions on box for a 9×13-inch pan and cool completely. This may be done up to a day ahead.

② With a round cookie cutter, slightly smaller circumference than the jars, cut out 8-10 cake circles.

③ Alternate layers of cake and ice cream in the jars, starting with cake and ending with ice cream. Garnish with sprinkles, secure lid, and freeze until ready to serve.

BLUSH-OF-PINK LEMONADE ICE CREAM

Mistakes were made. Faces were fallen flat on. Secrets were revealed at precisely the wrong moment. Gasses escaped publicly from places whence gasses should only escape in private. Shirts were worn inside out. Names were mispronounced or even forgotten.

Sure, you'll laugh about this one day. But today is not that day.

If you're not ready to savor your rosy-cheeked experience, savor the flavor of this Blush-of-Pink Lemonade Ice Cream.

Prep time: 5 minutes
Chill and process time: 2-3 hours
Makes 1½ quarts

INGREDIENTS

1 cup whole milk
1 cup superfine sugar
1 teaspoon vanilla
2 cups heavy whipping cream
½ tin frozen pink lemonade concentrate
1-2 drops hot pink food coloring, paste, or gel

DIRECTIONS

① Whisk milk, sugar, and vanilla in stand mixer until sugar dissolves.

② Add cream, lemonade concentrate, and food coloring. Mix until well blended.

③ Process in ice cream maker according to manufacturer's directions.

④ Serve immediately for soft serve, or cover and freeze for 2-3 hours before serving.

CAN'T WAIT

BAD DAY № 3

PiNEAPPLE PATiENCE SPICY SORBET

You ordered your new iPhone 99XG two weeks ago and it was due to arrive yesterday.

Your whole life will change with the slick, new, almost-the-same-but-better design; the screen with more pixels than your eyes can process; and enough memory to store every single episode of your favorite cooking competition.

This morning the tracking said, "Out for Delivery." You postponed your shower. You let your breakfast cereal get mushy, lest your joyous crunching drown out the sound of the doorbell. You swore off trips to the restroom. Yet somehow, when you stepped outside to water your petunias, you found a note stuck to the front door: "Delivery attempted. No answer."

What kind of UPS ninja tomfoolery is this?!

Whether you're waiting for your acceptance letter from Harvard or can't bear the slowness of the countdown to Christmas, there are times when the waiting game can be excruciating. Distraction is your friend here. Throw yourself into a complicated project, call a friend for a chat, or make this delicious Pineapple Patience Spicy Sorbet.

Prep time: 10 minutes

Chill and process time: 2-3 hours (optional—especially if you *really* can't wait!)

Makes 1 ½ quarts

INGREDIENTS

1 large pineapple, peeled, cored, and cut into 2-inch chunks

1 teaspoon fresh ginger, grated

2 tablespoons honey or maple syrup, or to taste

⅛ teaspoon cayenne pepper

Pinch of salt

DIRECTIONS

① Place pineapple chunks in the freezer to chill.

② Blend all ingredients in a blender or food processor until very smooth.

③ Taste the puree and add more sweetener if needed.

④ Process in ice cream maker according to manufacturer's directions.

⑤ Serve immediately for soft serve, or cover and freeze for 2-3 hours before serving.

21

BAD DAY Nº 4

OVERWHELMED, OVERSTIMULATED, AND UNDER SIEGE!

CHILL-OUT VANILLA ICE CREAM

Road trips, birthday parties, conferences, company-wide meetings, or summer vacations with the kids.

These things can be fun. And you like fun. But then the fun is *just too much!*

The sounds and colors and movement in the world make you want to scream. But you can't scream, even for ice cream, because it would only add to the noise pollution.

You want noise-canceling headphones and a space suit, or to sit at the bottom of a deserted swimming pool with your eyes closed.

No more jostling in crowded elevators. No more people asking whether you're done yet or if they can have a Popsicle or if you've seen their shoes or if you would turn up the AC.

Stop. Take a breath, find a quiet place, and chill out with the ice cream that all other ice creams aspire to be: Vanilla. It's mature. It's classy. It's blessedly simple. Think of it as your own personal sensory deprivation chamber in a bowl. Boring never tasted so good.

And if you want to hide in the broom closet wearing ear plugs while you eat it, who are we to judge?

Prep time: 10 minutes
Chill and process time: 2-3 hours
Makes 1½ quarts

INGREDIENTS

2 cups heavy whipping cream	¾ cup sugar
	2 teaspoons vanilla
2 cups whole milk	Pinch of salt

DIRECTIONS

1. In a large bowl, whisk together all ingredients until the sugar is dissolved and (if using) vanilla bean paste is incorporated.

2. Carefully pour ice cream base into a 1-gallon zip-close freezer bag and seal securely. Lay flat in the freezer for at least 2 hours or until ready to use.

3. When the mixture is frozen, you have three options:

    ⓐ Remove from freezer and crumble into frozen ice cream pieces. Eat immediately.

    ⓑ Remove from freezer and crumble. Blend in a food processor until creamy and smooth—soft serve ice cream at its finest!

    ⓒ Remove from freezer and crumble. Blend in a food processor until creamy and smooth. Pour the mixture into a freezer-safe storage container and freeze until firm, about 2 hours. Remove from freezer 10 minutes before serving.

BAD DAY
Nº.5

BLACK THUMB

FLOWERPOT ICE CREAM DESSERT

You can kill a cactus. You have killed several, in fact. You've somehow managed to under-water some and over-water others. No plant is safe in your care.

When you look at the luscious produce spilling forth from your neighbor's garden, you think, "That looks easy. I should plant a garden." But after spending one hundred dollars on dirt and a summer of care and watering, all you have to show for it is some sad kale leaves and one pitiful pepper.

You can try again next year, maybe with the help of that neighbor. In the meantime, help yourself to a garden that looks divine and tastes a heck of a lot better than your neighbor's prize cabbage. Is her garden made with marshmallows? Does her dirt taste like chocolate? We didn't think so.

Prep time: 15 minutes
Makes 4 servings

INGREDIENTS

- 4 (2-inch) clay flowerpots
- 4 large marsh-mallows or 4 small pieces of cake
- 1 pint ice cream, sorbet, or frozen yogurt, any flavor
- Chocolate syrup
- Sprinkles
- 2 drinking straws, cut in half
- 4 fresh or silk flowers

DIRECTIONS

① Wash and dry clay pots.

② Place marshmallow or piece of cake in the bottom of each clay pot. Press down, making sure it covers the hole in the bottom of the pot.

③ Put a scoop of ice cream into each flowerpot and drizzle with chocolate syrup. Decorate with sprinkles and insert a straw into the center. Place the flower stem inside the straw.

④ Serve immediately, or store covered in the freezer before inserting flowers into straws.

PARKED ON
THE FREEWAY

BAD DAY
NO. 6

RASPBERRY TRAFFIC JAM SWIRL ICE CREAM

There's no construction, no accident. But for some reason traffic has come to a complete stop. Why doesn't everyone understand that if you all just started driving at the same time, there would be no traffic jam?

But they don't understand. And so you sit in a sea of cars, on the road to rage. You don't devolve into a horn honking, rude gesturing jerk hole. Not on the outside. You turn up your podcast and try to ignore your mounting frustration.

You stare straight ahead and breathe through your panic. You will be late for that dog grooming appointment, and Sadie needs to get her hair done! They'll have to rush her through. Again.

It's time to turn to a jam that won't leave you flustered and with a substandard doggie do. Once Sadie has her mullet, head home for a taste of Raspberry Traffic Jam Swirl Ice Cream. It's fruity to symbolize how *crazy* bad traffic makes us, paired with calming vanilla as a sedative. Ahhh. This is a jam you'll be happy to savor.

Prep time: 15 minutes
Chill time: 4-6 hours
Makes 1 ½ quarts

INGREDIENTS

¾ cup sweetened condensed milk
1 teaspoon vanilla
1 cup fresh raspberries
1¼ cups heavy whipping cream

DIRECTIONS

① In a small bowl, whisk together sweetened condensed milk and vanilla.

② Puree raspberries in a blender or food processor, then strain through a sieve into a bowl, discarding seeds. Set aside until ready to use.

③ Whip the cream until stiff peaks form, then combine with condensed milk base. Stir well to combine.

④ Pour mixture into a loaf pan, then drizzle raspberry puree over the mixture and swirl with a knife.

⑤ Cover with plastic wrap and chill 4-6 hours or overnight.

BAD DAY Nº. 7

DISHEVELED DOMESTICITY

MUD PiES

Prep time: 10 minutes
Freeze time: 2-3 hours
Makes 6-8 servings

INGREDIENTS

- 7-8 whole graham crackers, or 20-25 vanilla wafers or ginger snaps, or 15-20 chocolate cream wafer cookies, crushed
- 4 tablespoons butter, melted
- 4 mini pie pans or 1 (9-inch) pie pan
- 1 pint vanilla ice cream, softened
- 1 pint coffee or caramel ice cream, softened
- 1 pint chocolate ice cream, softened
- Whipped cream
- Fudge ice cream topping
- 2 (1 gallon) plastic zip-close bags

DIRECTIONS

① Empty cookie crumbs into a medium bowl and stir in melted butter.

② Press equal amounts of crumbs into 4 mini pie pans or one 9 inch pie pan.

③ Chill in freezer for about 15-20 minutes.

④ Scoop the softened vanilla ice cream into pans first. Top with the coffee or caramel ice cream, then the chocolate ice cream. Make sure to smooth the ice cream between each layer. This is your "mud."

⑤ Garnish with whipped cream and a drizzle of fudge, then freeze for 2-3 hours before serving.

A ccording to the law, you own that house. Well, you and the bank. Mostly the bank. It's complicated.

But you know for certain that the house doesn't own you. How, then, have things gotten so out of control? You can blame the kids—and, sure, they did leave Skittles on the piano. But blame doesn't really help anyone.

Besides, whose tools are still sitting all over the floor in the garage, rendering it unusable? Whose jacket is draped over the dining room chair? Those would be yours, my friend.

Life is busy and little things add up, and that's okay. We do our best and leave the rest. So, you haven't mopped the floor in longer than you'd care to admit to your mother-in-law. But if you add up all the good things you've done while that floor was getting dirty, you'll realize a little dirt isn't such a bad thing.

And sometimes a little *mud* can be a great thing. Celebrate the crazy messiness of life with an intentionally crafted, chocolatey perfect Mud Pie.

BAD DAY

Nº. 8

BORED OUT
Of YOUR MinD

DiVERTING DONUT SUNDAE

Prep time: 5 minutes
Makes 1 sundae

INGREDIENTS

Frosted donut
  with sprinkles
Ice cream, any
  flavor
Chocolate sauce

Whipped cream
Maraschino
  cherry
Sprinkles

DIRECTIONS

① Place donut in a shallow bowl, then top with a scoop of your favorite ice cream.

② Drizzle with chocolate sauce and a dollop of whipped cream.

③ Garnish with a cherry and sprinkles.

W hen you were a kid, your mom told you, "Only boring people get bored." And you thought, *That's not possible, because I am amazing and I'm so bored right now I actually cannot handle my life. ENTERTAIN ME!*

But now you're an adult, so boredom should never strike. There's too much to do, and be, and experience. Your phone alone should be able to keep you occupied for hours.

However, sometimes between the working out and the social media and the Netflix and the knitting, you just get sick of it all. You can think of a thousand things to do, but you just don't *feel* like doing any of them.

You want to yell, "MOM! I'm BORED!" and have her bring you a treat. But she lives in Indiana and there are no treats in your house. But there could be. If you made them.

In the absence of your mother, take our unqualified medical advice and craft a Diverting Donut Sundae. They're simple to make and always exciting to eat, the perfect remedy for a boring day.

YAPPY CANINE NEIGHBOR

BAD DAY
Nº. 9

ALMOST-FRIED ICE CREAM

The dog was so cute until she opened her mouth. And then it's been nothing but *yap, yap, yap* ever since. You're unloading the groceries? How dare you! You're working in your garden? The absolute nerve!

That little nipper hates your very existence. And, rest assured, the feeling is mutual. There's a special kind of headache that dawns with an unrelenting bark fest and your head has been pounding for a week.

You've asked the neighbors what you could do to make the dog more at ease. You've tried speaking calm words, commanding sharply, and even bribing her with treats. It's no use. This dog is determined to drive you out of the neighborhood. Your nerves are fried!

And your ice cream can be too. Will it shut the dog up? No. Will it distract you so you can better ignore her? Absolutely.

Prep time: 15 minutes
Freeze time: 15 minutes
Makes 4-6 servings

INGREDIENTS

1 pint ice cream (Vanilla is classic, but chocolate or coffee are delish!)

1¼ cups corn flakes cereal, crushed

½ teaspoon ground cinnamon

2 tablespoons butter, melted

2 teaspoons granulated sugar

Whipped cream

Sprinkles (optional)

Maraschino cherries

DIRECTIONS

① Line a small sheet pan with parchment paper and place in freezer.

② Scoop ice cream into 4-6 equal-sized balls and place on prepared pan in freezer.

③ In a medium saucepan, combine crushed corn cereal, cinnamon, and melted butter. Cook, stirring occasionally, until the cereal turns golden brown, 5-7 minutes.

④ Remove from heat and stir in sugar. Transfer to a shallow bowl and let cool.

⑤ Remove ice cream balls from freezer and roll in cereal mixture.

⑥ To serve, garnish with whipped cream, sprinkles, and a cherry. To prep ahead, roll in cereal mixture and freeze, covered, until ready to use. Then garnish and serve.

BOOK
SERIES
WITHDRAWAL

CUPCAKE BATTER iCE CREAM

For the last eight books of your reading life, you've grown attached to some pretty amazing characters. In some ways, they're more real than your actual friends, because they live *inside* of you. You carry them and their stories with you wherever you go, and you always hope that good things will come to them in the future.

But the series is over. The books are done. Effectively, your favorite author has killed the plucky group of adventurers who helped you through middle school.

Does Angerson ever learn to use his fish powers effectively? You'll never know. Will Wanda Vladios ever tell Carshedore how she feels about his cooking? It's all dust in the wind. The last page has been read, the final book has been closed, and life will never be the same.

The book series needed to end, but some things are better left undone. A delicious spoonful of cookie dough or cupcake batter, for example, can taste even more delicious than the real thing. In our rich and decadent Cupcake Batter Ice Cream, we've captured the flavor of an unbaked cake without the danger of raw ingredients. And if you're sad when your bowl comes to an end, you can always dish up another tomorrow.

Prep time: 10 minutes
Chill and process time: 2-3 hours
Makes 1 ½ quarts

INGREDIENTS

- 1½ cups heavy whipping cream
- 1½ cups half and half
- 1 cup superfine sugar
- Pinch of salt
- 1 teaspoon vanilla
- 1 teaspoon almond extract
- ½ teaspoon butter extract
- 2 purchased vanilla cupcakes (with vanilla frosting), crumbled
- ½ cup rainbow sprinkles

DIRECTIONS

① In a large bowl, combine whipping cream, half and half, sugar, and salt. Stir until sugar is dissolved.

② Add vanilla, almond, and butter extracts. Mix well.

③ Pour into prepared ice cream maker and process according to manufacturer's instructions.

④ After 10 minutes, check to see if ice cream has begun to solidify. If not, wait 2-3 minutes. Then add the crumbled cupcakes and sprinkles and continue to process until desired soft serve consistency. Total churn time takes approximately 20 minutes.

⑤ Serve immediately for soft serve, or cover and freeze for 2-3 hours before serving.

CHAPTER TWO

MODERATE TRAUMA

Unrequited love, shattering election results, homesickness—all of these can make for a pretty terrible day. In this section, we're graduating from run-of-the-mill, sleep-it-off irritation to moderate levels of actual trauma.

To cope with these rough days, you may need the help of a loved one or the formulation of an actual plan to make things better. Everything might not just "look better" after a good night's sleep.

With the added level of mental and emotional work needed to get through these hard times, you may enjoy desserts with a little more *oomph*. Ingredients like cream cheese, peanut butter, and coconut milk may need to be administered.

BAD DAY
№. 11

WAITING FOR MR. DARCY TO GET A CLUE

CREAM CHEESY iCE CREAM

L ove everlasting.

Romantic comedies make it look inevitable. It's not a question of "if," but "when." Either you will suddenly recognize the amazing man who's been waiting patiently in your life and ride off into the sunset together, or he will finally notice *you*.

Why is it, then, that you've been waiting with your eyes wide open for years and Mr. Darcy shows zero signs of boarding the clue bus? You are kind. You are strong. You are beautiful. You are worthy of love.

Are thoughts of romance nothing but cheesy, impossible fairy tales? Maybe. But real, true, lasting love is not. People make it happen every day.

And what's so wrong with cheesy? While you're waiting for crazy, impossible, cheesy, amazing love to hit you in the face, insert a little creamy, cheesy, frozen deliciousness into your mouth.

Prep time: 10 minutes
Chill time: 8 hours
Process time: 20 minutes
Makes 1½ quarts

INGREDIENTS

- 3 cups half and half
- 1¼ cups powdered sugar
- 2 egg yolks
- 1 package (8 ounces) cream cheese, room temperature, cut into small pieces
- 2 teaspoons vanilla
- Fresh berries or fruit of choice, or Shake-It-Off Strawberry Sauce on page 111

DIRECTIONS

① Whisk together half and half, powdered sugar, and egg yolks in a saucepan. Cook over medium heat whisking constantly, 8-10 minutes, or until mixture thickens slightly.

② Remove from heat and whisk in cream cheese and vanilla until completely melted.

③ Let cool, then cover and chill in refrigerator 2-3 hours or overnight. It may be a good idea to prepare this base the day before you need it.

④ Pour chilled mixture into an electric ice cream maker and process according to manufacturer's directions.

⑤ Serve immediately for soft serve, or cover and freeze for 2-3 hours before serving. Garnish with fresh berries or Shake-It-Off Strawberry Sauce.

BAD DAY Nº. 12

FOOT IN MOUTH

NO-REGRETS PEANUT BUTTER ICE CREAM

" *D*id I really just say that!?"
It's not always easy to think before you speak, but if you're like us, you've spent hours of your life thinking *after* you've spoken— obsessing, even.

Words are so powerful and can do endless good. They can also hurt, shame, or embarrass. If you're feeling sad today because you've said something you regret, come up with a plan to fix it.

If there's no good way to take back what you said without causing more damage, you may just need to suck it up and move on. You'll do better next time, right?

Putting your foot in your mouth is no fun. So, remove your foot and insert a spoonful of No-Regrets Peanut Butter Ice Cream. The gooey, chewy peanut butter will keep your mouth so busy you won't be able to relapse.

Prep time: 15 minutes
Freeze time: 2–3 hours
Makes 6–8 servings

INGREDIENTS

1 can (14 ounces) sweetened condensed milk
½ cup creamy peanut butter
2 cups heavy whipping cream, whipped
1 bag (8 ounces) Reese's Mini Peanut Butter cups, sliced in half
1 cup marshmallow cream, purchased or homemade (try our Optimistic Marshmallow Sauce on page 117)
Shake-It-Off Strawberry Sauce (page 111)

DIRECTIONS

① In a large bowl, whisk together the sweetened condensed milk and peanut butter.

② Gently stir the whipped cream into the peanut butter mixture, then fold in peanut butter cups.

③ Pour half the mixture into a freezer-safe bowl. Drop half the marshmallow cream on top and swirl with a knife.

④ Spoon the rest of the peanut butter mixture on top and top with the remaining marshmallow cream. Freeze for 2–3 hours or overnight.

⑤ Scoop into bowls and serve with Shake-It-Off Strawberry Sauce.

BAD DAY Nº. 13

DEMOCRACY in ACTION

SWEET BLUES-BERRY "NICE" CREAM

We don't always get what we want. Maybe you came up aces in the mayoral race, but that jerk-bucket robot won the school board election. There's rarely an election in which everything goes your way.

So, on Election Day, you probably find yourself happy-mad. You celebrate the gift of democracy and all the ways your dreams came true, and you mourn the passing of a ballot initiative that makes keeping giraffes as pets illegal.

On Election Day, choose to have this on tap. It's a combination of all the feels with just enough sweet to balance out the blues. Sweet Blues-Berry Ice Cream can help you navigate the returns.

Prep time: 5 minutes
Freeze time: 2-3 hours
Makes 3-4 servings

INGREDIENTS

3 cups blueberries, frozen

2 tablespoons agave or honey, to taste

1 teaspoon lemon zest

3 tablespoons fresh lemon juice

⅓ cup water

DIRECTIONS

① Blend frozen blueberries, sweetener of choice, lemon zest, lemon juice, and water in a food processor until smooth and creamy.

② Taste and add sweetener if needed.

③ Serve immediately for soft serve, or cover and freeze for 2-3 hours before serving.

BAD DAY
Nº 14

DATELESS

CHEER-UP CHOCOLATE COCONUT MILK ICE CREAM

Prep time: 5 minutes
Freeze time: 2-3 hours
Makes 4 servings

INGREDIENTS

1 can (14 ounces) full-fat coconut milk

¼ cup and 2 tablespoons cocoa powder

¼ cup honey or maple syrup

1 teaspoon vanilla

1 teaspoon chocolate extract

DIRECTIONS

1. Combine ingredients in a blender, and blend until smooth and creamy.

2. Serve immediately for soft serve, or cover and freeze for 2-3 hours before serving.

"*I*'m the only one without a date to the company Christmas party!"

You know it's not a true statement, but it sure feels true, and it sends you straight back to your insecure adolescence.

The prom.

You watched couple after annoying couple walk arm in arm through the halls of your high school, making plans for the dance. And all you got was a date with your mom to play Settlers of Catan.

Don't get me wrong, Catan with moms is *ah-mazing*. But the prom sounded pretty okay too. And you didn't go.

Now you're an adult and you have a choice to make. Maybe it would be more fun trading wheat for sheep in your PJs if Cheer-Up Chocolate Coconut Milk Ice Cream were also a commodity at the table.

Or maybe it would be even more fun to get glammed up and go to the party solo, and then enjoy some ice cream to celebrate your maturity and confidence. Either way, you can't go wrong with chocolate and coconut milk.

OUT Of TIME

BAD DAY
Nº. 15

QUICK-AS-A-WINK ICE CREAM TREAT

It's like a giant stopwatch is hanging over your head. You've got a million things to do and not nearly enough time to do them.

So you run around like a headless chicken, desperately trying to cram as much as you can into a day that stubbornly won't stretch a second longer than twenty-four hours.

And the giant stopwatch keeps ticking. You're out of time. You need to do some triage.

Make a batch of these Quick-as-a-Wink Ice Cream Treats, sit down with one for five minutes, and circle the most important items on your to-do list. Then figure out which ones you can outsource and which ones you actually have to complete yourself. Only the essentials stay.

Although not *essential*, this dessert can help set the tone going forward because it's no frills, like your day needs to be.

Prep time: 5 minutes
Makes 4-6 servings

INGREDIENTS

1 pint vanilla ice cream

1 pint fruit sorbet, any flavor

Fresh fruit for garnish

DIRECTIONS

① Inside a small cup or ¼ pint mason jar, make three layers; start and end with vanilla ice cream, with fruit sorbet in the middle.

② Garnish with fresh fruit of choice.

③ Eat immediately for soft-serve style, or freeze until firm, about 1 hour.

BAD DAY
№. 16

HOMESICK

GiNGERBREAD HOME ICE CREAM

Prep time: 5 minutes
Freeze time: 2–3 hours
Makes 2 quarts

INGREDIENTS

- ½ gallon vanilla ice cream, softened
- 1 teaspoon cinnamon, ground
- 1 teaspoon ginger, ground
- ¼ teaspoon cardamom, ground
- ¼ teaspoon cloves, ground
- ¼ teaspoon nutmeg, freshly grated
- 2 tablespoons molasses
- Gingerbread figures (optional)

DIRECTIONS

① Place softened ice cream into a large bowl. Stir in spices and molasses.

② Cover and freeze for 2–3 hours before serving. Serve with a small gingerbread boy or other figures.

*D*orothy knows there's no place like home. Deep down, you know it too. Maybe home is a physical location for you, that green house on the cul-de-sac in Saskatoon. Perhaps home for you is wherever your dad lives and churns out his famous chocolate chip pancakes.

Did you wake up today and realize it's been far too long since you felt that warm, safe, relaxed feeling of home-ness? Do you need your parents or your blankie or your favorite backyard tree in the worst way?

Well, call someone who loves you, and then get out all the heartwarming spices that conjure up memories of pumpkin pie and gingerbread and warm apple cider by a crackling fire. Make your snack time feel like a little taste of home this afternoon.

You may be far from the place you love most, but Gingerbread Home Ice Cream will always be there for you.

BLACKENED CASSEROLE À LA SMOKE

BLACK MAGIC MINT ICE CREAM

Generally, when your food turns black, you can't eat it anymore. And it smells bad. And it fills you with rage, because you spent time and money to create something delicious for your family, only to throw it all in the garbage.

Cabbage is probably the worst, but any dinner burnt to a crisp is a major suck. And then there's nothing to eat and you have to start all over. In cases like this, we generally let the pizza man take over. He seems to enjoy it and the kids prefer it to cabbage, even the properly cooked variety.

As a remedy for your dinner disaster, try a dessert that proves black is beautiful. This Black Magic Mint Ice Cream has the color of fine licorice and the wintery fresh bite of mint. Its chill will reassure you that the black is not from burnination, and its smooth texture will remind you that you're a pretty great cook . . . most of the time.

Prep time: 10 minutes
Chill and process time: 2-3 hours
Makes 1 quart

INGREDIENTS

2 cups heavy whipping cream
1 cup milk
⅔ cup sugar
¼ cup food-grade activated charcoal powder*
Pinch of salt
1½ teaspoon vanilla
1½ teaspoon peppermint extract

*Food-grade activated charcoal powder is made from coconut ash and imparts a black color, but adds no flavor to foods. It can be purchased on Amazon.

DIRECTIONS

① In a small saucepan, bring whipping cream, milk, and sugar to a simmer, stirring to dissolve the sugar. When sugar has dissolved, remove from heat and whisk in activated charcoal, salt, vanilla, and peppermint extract.

② Transfer to a bowl, cover, and refrigerate until cold, 2-3 hours, or up to 1 day.

③ Pour chilled mixture into ice cream maker and process according to manufacturer's directions.

④ Serve immediately for soft serve, or cover and freeze for 2-3 hours before serving.

BAD DAY
№. 18

OVERSLEPT

1-2-3 VANiLLA iCE CREAM FOR ME

Prep time: 5 minutes
Freeze time: 4-6 hours
Makes 1 ½ pints

INGREDIENTS

1 can (14 ounces) sweetened condensed milk

2 teaspoons vanilla

Pinch of salt

2 cups heavy whipping cream

DIRECTIONS

① In a medium bowl, stir together sweetened condensed milk, vanilla, and a pinch of salt.

② In a large bowl, beat cream on high with an electric mixer until stiff peaks form.

③ Gently fold whipped cream into condensed milk mixture and pour into a freezable container, like a loaf pan.

④ Freeze 4-6 hours and remove from freezer a few minutes before serving.

Your hair is crazy. Your stomach is empty. You ran out the door for work with just seconds to spare. Sleeping in late feels so good while you're lying in your pillow palace. But when you finally stop hitting snooze and realize you are truly, deeply late for work, the luxurious comfort evaporates.

Sleeping in can ruin the entire day, as you arrive a few minutes late and a few steps behind for every appointment all day long. How will you ever catch up?

We can save you a few minutes.

When you're making dessert tonight, opt for the simplest ice cream recipe around: 1-2-3 Vanilla Ice Cream for Me. With such a short prep time, you'll make up all the time you lost this morning and it will be like you never slept in at all! You're welcome.

BAD DAY № 19

FIRST LOSER

ICE CREAM VICTORY CUPCAKES

Sometimes close just isn't good enough. You lose the election by four votes. The person in line ahead of you orders the last double chocolate donut. Your boss tells you she gave the promotion to Rebecca, but it was *really* close.

You almost had it. That should feel good, right? But somehow, "almost" feels worse than "not even close." You can smell the victory, but you'll never get to taste it.

It's time to turn to a dessert that will be a feast for all of your senses. With these Ice Cream Victory Cupcakes, you'll see the colors, you'll smell the aroma, and this time all your hard work will pay off, because the flavor will be absolutely delicious.

There's no coming in second this time. You'll be winning at ice cream.

Prep time for cupcake assembly: 15 minutes
Freeze time: 2-3 hours
Makes 24 cupcakes

INGREDIENTS

24 cupcakes, unfrosted, any flavor, purchased or homemade ahead of time
½ gallon ice cream, softened, any flavor

Whipped cream
M&M's, Skittles, or sprinkles
24 maraschino cherries

DIRECTIONS

① With a melon baller or teaspoon, hollow out the top center of each cupcake and fill with ice cream.

② Place on sheet pan, cover with plastic wrap and freeze 2-3 hours or overnight. Alternately, garnish and serve immediately for a soft serve consistency.

③ To serve, top with whipped cream, candies, and sprinkles. Garnish with a cherry.

BAD DAY
№ 20

DRIVER'S ED
DRAMA

WATERMELON VACATION

Prep time: 15 minutes
Freeze time: 2-3 hours (optional)
Makes 4-6 parfaits

INGREDIENTS

1 pint pistachio ice cream or lime sherbet	1 pint strawberry or raspberry sorbet
1 pint vanilla ice cream	½ cup milk chocolate chips

DIRECTIONS

① In a parfait glass, layer pistachio ice cream or lime sherbet, vanilla ice cream, and strawberry or raspberry sorbet.

② Garnish with chocolate chips. This dish can be served immediately, but for better presentation and for the layers to hold their shape, first cover and freeze until ready to serve.

Have you ever taught a teenager to drive? Have you ever taken a two year old to an antiques store and then followed her around, gently reminding her not to touch the china? The experiences are similar. The fear is real.

The main difference is that if the driver messes up, she could kill someone. So, you hand her the keys to your fully loaded weapon of a vehicle and then sit beside her, gently reminding her not to have a head-on collision or run a stop sign or steamroll a pedestrian.

There is no routine task in parenting quite as traumatic as teaching a child to drive. And not just for the parent. The teen—if she's smart—is terrified, too. The first two weeks shave four years off your life.

You need a distraction, something to take you back to the lazy days of summer, when you were young and carefree, running through the sand and spitting watermelon seeds off a bridge.

This watermelon dessert is as adorable as your student driver's baby photos and as sweet as the relief of pulling safely into your garage each afternoon.

BAD DAY № 21

A TRIP TO CRAZY TOWN

NUTS-FOR-PISTACHIO ICE CREAM

You're not the crazy one. You know you're not. But neither do you feel sane or in control. It's possible that someone in your life is driving you bonkers. It's possible that your kids or your spouse or your dubstep blasting neighbors are driving you nuts.

And why do we even use that word as a negative? Nuts. Why, nuts are some of our very best friends—cashews, almonds, pistachios. Ah, yes. Pistachios. Mmm.

Take a few bites of an ice cream that reminds you how delicious nuts can be. And buy ear plugs.

Prep time: 30 minutes
Chill and process time: 2-3 hours
Makes 1 ½ quarts

INGREDIENTS

1 cup pistachios, unsalted and shelled
¾ cup sugar, divided into ½ cup and ¼ cup
2 cups whole milk
½ teaspoon almond extract
4 large egg yolks
1 cup heavy whipping cream
¾ cup pistachios, unsalted, shelled, toasted, and chopped

DIRECTIONS

① Process 1 cup pistachios with ¼ cup sugar in food processor.

② In a saucepan, bring milk and pistachio mixture to boil. Remove from heat and stir in almond extract.

③ Whisk egg yolks and remaining ½ cup sugar in medium bowl. Gradually whisk into hot milk mixture.

④ Return saucepan to stove. Cook over low heat, stirring constantly until custard thickens and coats the back of spoon, about 10 minutes (do not boil).

⑤ Strain cooked ice cream base into a sieve over a large bowl. Cover and chill 2 hours or overnight.

⑥ Before processing in an ice cream maker, stir in heavy whipping cream and chopped pistachios. Process in ice cream maker according to manufacturer's directions.

⑦ Serve immediately for soft serve, or cover and freeze for 2-3 hours before serving.

BAD DAY
№ 22

GREEN WITH ENVY

SOUR GRAPE SORBETTO

Prep time: 10 minutes

Chill and process time: 2-3 hours (optional)

> Note: To shorten prep time, make simple syrup and sorbetto base 1 day ahead.

Makes approximately 1 quart

Have you spent too much time on social media this week? If you've built a semi-permanent residence in the land of eternal vacations, smiling children, and flawless kitchen remodels, your life might start to seem shabby in comparison.

Logically, you know that for every perfect photo of little Harrison slam-dunking in his pre-K basketball league, he likely fell flat on his face twenty or thirty times. But it's easy to compare his Insta-MVP moment to the game-day failures of your athletically challenged spawn.

And if your kitchen is still stuck in the eighties, you might flush green with envy at the sight of your friend's new marble countertops. Never mind that you spent your renovation money on a fabulous trip to Europe. In this moment, all you can see is what you lack.

Step one, put the phone away.

Step two, pull out your blender.

Step three, eat a little Sour Grape Sorbetto instead. Because sour grapes can be delightful, but only in your mouth. If you're comparing your life to others', you'll end up with nothing but hurt.

INGREDIENTS

¾ cup maple syrup
¾ cup water
2 sprigs fresh thyme or lemon thyme
3 cups grape juice, purple

DIRECTIONS

① Make a simple syrup by heating the maple syrup and water in a small saucepan. Add thyme and simmer 10 minutes, stirring occasionally.

② Cool and remove thyme. Stir in grape juice.

③ Cover and chill for 2-3 hours or overnight.

④ Process in ice cream maker according to manufacturer's directions.

⑤ Serve immediately for soft serve, or cover and freeze for 2-3 hours before serving.

BAD DAY
Nº. 23

SOMEONE ELSE'S
SCIENCE FAIR

NERDS NIGHTMARE ICE CREAM

Prep time: 10 minutes
Freeze time: 2-3 hours
Makes 4-6 servings

INGREDIENTS

1 pint vanilla ice cream, softened

1 box (5 ounces) Rainbow Nerds

½ cup white chocolate chips

DIRECTIONS

① In a bowl, combine softened ice cream, Nerds, and white chocolate chips and stir to combine.

② Cover and freeze for 2-3 hours before serving.

③ Serve with additional Nerds as garnish.

Have you ever found yourself awake at midnight, "helping" arrange a science fair display board for a fourth grader? It's most definitely not your project, so why are you holding the glue?

And it's not just about conducting an experiment. This project needs to be done to *exact* specifications. Labels the wrong font size? How dare you!

Whether it's a science fair, a PTA fundraiser, or assisting a colleague with a challenging work deadline, sometimes you get roped into someone else's nightmare.

You just like to help out. And when they get the blue ribbon or the volunteer of the year award or the big promotion, you will be happy for them.

But you deserve something for *you*. Keeping with the science fair theme, reward your inner nerd for her part in the victory with a generous helping of Nerds Nightmare Ice Cream. If you can't handle all that goodness, ask your friend to give you a hand eating it. It's the least she can do.

CHAPTER THREE

WORST DAY EVER

*I*n your life, you will probably experience more than one WORST DAY EVER! Your current terrible day often feels like the worst ever because it's the one you're experiencing *right now*. You feel the injustice (or painful justice) of your speeding ticket the moment you get pulled over. The throbbing of your sprained ankle is ever-present. Waking up to see your beloved goldfish floating in his glass palace is so real and fresh.

These painful realities plant you right in the middle of the worst day ever. And you have very little control over these events as they unfold. You can choose to drive slower in the future or watch where you're stepping to avoid injury. You can even invest in a better aquarium filtration system next time to prolong the life of your fish-baby.

But in the moment, you really just need to feel the pain. And pain tastes better with a little ice cream to sweeten it up.

BAD DAY
№. 24

SPEEDING
TICKET

PEDAL-TO-THE-METAL PARFAIT

We're happy to accept most tickets into our lives—raffle tickets, season tickets to the Seahawks, front row tickets to *Hamilton*. Seeing one of these tickets sparks joy and lets us know that good things are coming our way.

But there's one kind of ticket that has no business being associated with the rest of ticketdom.

A speeding ticket.

You're just zooming along, minding your own business, trying to get to the orthodontist on time, when suddenly you see lights in your rearview mirror. And before you know it, an officer of the law is offering you a ticket to nowhere good.

Day ruined.

If you love speed but decide all this law breaking and fine paying isn't for you, try this lightning-fast parfait. As one of the quickest and easiest recipes in the book, it provides the speed you crave at a fraction of the emotional and financial cost.

Prep time: 5 minutes
Makes 1 parfait

INGREDIENTS

2 scoops chocolate ice cream

¼ cup Reese's Pieces Candies

Canned whipped cream

4-6 Reese's Peanut Butter Cup Miniatures

INSTRUCTIONS

① In a large glass jar, layer chocolate ice cream, Reese's Pieces, whipped cream, and Reese's Peanut Butter Cups. Continue until you reach the top of the jar.

② Top with whipped cream and garnish with additional Reese's Pieces.

③ Enjoy a perfect parfait for a speedy recovery!

KLUTZY
CONSEQUENCES

BAD DAY
No. 25

CHOCO-BANANA RECOVERY POPS

*I*t all happened so fast. Your brain knew your thumb should get out of the way, right as you chopped the veggie knife down on top of it. But your big old opposable digit was just too slow. And it got harmed.

Or maybe you ran for three miles in the glorious autumn sunshine, with the wind gently ruffling your perfect ponytail as the leaves fell around you in a spectacular shower. And then you lost your footing on the stairs to your apartment and you twisted your ankle.

You wish you could rewind the clock thirty seconds and have a do-over. Then you wouldn't have a useless hand wrapped in gauze or be stuck on the couch with an ice pack.

If you can only get up for a few minutes at a time, spend just a few minutes of hands on time crafting these Choco-Banana Recovery Pops and then rest your recovering appendage while the freezer does all the work. Do you have bananas? Chocolate? Coconut oil? We're about to make all of your dreams come true.

Prep time: 5 minutes
Freeze time: 2-3 hours
Makes 4 pops

INGREDIENTS

- 4 Popsicle or craft sticks
- 2 bananas, peeled and halved crosswise
- Homemade "Magic Shell," page 119
- ½ cup chopped nuts, dried fruit, coconut, or sprinkles
- ½ cup crushed graham cracker, ginger snap, vanilla wafer, or chocolate cookie crumbs

DIRECTIONS

① Insert a Popsicle stick into the cut end of each banana half.

② Cover with foil and freeze 2-3 hours or overnight. (Foil-covered frozen bananas will stay perfect in the freezer for up to 3 months. Great to keep in stock for quick snacks.)

③ Following the Homemade "Magic Shell" recipe, combine 3 parts chocolate chips to 1 part coconut oil. Microwave in 30 second intervals until melted, stirring each time.

④ Remove bananas from freezer, unwrap, and spoon "Magic Shell" over each banana, then quickly roll or sprinkle in garnish of choice.

GOLDfish FUNERAL

RAINBOW SPRINKLES OF HOPE, CAKE, AND ICE CREAM

The beloved family goldfish has died. The circle of life is verifiably real and you feel it keenly. As you gather around the toilet before flushing him off to Davy Jones's locker, you pause to say a few words.

"Errol was a true friend. He lived his life like he ate his fish flakes: passionately and with undulating sucking motions. Never an unkind word did he speak. If all fish had been, and were, and ever would be like Errol, peace on Earth might be a reality."

After a moment of silence, you let him go. But you're left with questions. Is Errol's essence still with us? Is he happy right now? Will life ever be the same?

It's time to whip up some hope in a bowl. I suggest a batch of Rainbow Sprinkles of Hope, Cake, and Ice Cream. Send Errol off in style with a celebration of his life and accomplishments and a spoonful of sugar to help the funeral go down.

Prep time: 30 minutes
Chill and process time: 2-3 hours
Makes 1 ½ quarts

INGREDIENTS

2½ cups milk
2 cups heavy whipping cream
¾ cup sugar
½ cup Funfetti cake mix
Pinch of salt
5 large egg yolks
2 teaspoons vanilla
½ teaspoon almond extract
2 cups pound cake, cubed
⅓ cup rainbow sprinkles

DIRECTIONS

① Heat the milk, whipping cream, sugar, cake mix, and salt in a saucepan over medium heat, whisking until the sugar is dissolved completely.

② Whisk the egg yolks in a large bowl. Add about ½ cup of the warmed milk mixture to the yolks, stirring constantly to temper the eggs.

③ Add egg mixture into the remaining warmed milk mixture in the saucepan. Stir often over medium heat, until mixture coats the back of a spoon.

④ Remove from the heat and pour into a large bowl. Stir in vanilla and almond extracts.

⑤ Cover and chill 2-3 hours or overnight.

⑥ Pour cold mixture into ice cream maker and process according to manufacturer's directions.

⑦ After 10-15 minutes of processing, stop machine and add cake cubes and sprinkles. Continue until mixture is frozen.

⑧ Serve immediately for soft serve, or cover and freeze for 2-3 hours before serving.

TERRIBLE NEWS

BAD DAY
№ 27

BAD NEWS BERRIES SHERBET

Prep time: 10 minutes
Freeze time: 4 hours
Makes 4 cups

INGREDIENTS

3 cups frozen raspberries, strawberries, or blueberries

¼ cup fat-free condensed milk, or regular con- densed milk for a richer sherbet

Fresh berries, for garnish

Mint, for garnish

INSTRUCTIONS

① Combine the berries and the con- densed milk in a food processor or powerful blender and process until smooth and creamy.

② Transfer to an airtight container and freeze for 4 hours. If not scoopable after 4 hours, return to freezer for another hour.

③ Garnish with fresh berries and a sprig of mint.

*I*s the news real? Is it fake? All you know is that it sucks.

Maybe your mom left a message on your voice mail that simply said, "Call me," in that voice that never means, "Call me because I just found the cutest pink slippers at Ross!"

Or maybe you've spent too many hours watching news coverage of the latest celebrity breakup. *Not Liam and Taylor! I thought they had a forever love!*

Nearly every one of us remembers getting news that rocked our world. Whether you're feeling shocked, disheartened, or unsure how life will ever be the same, bad news is never a good thing—hence the name.

As you come to terms with what you've just heard, you may need to move on to another flavor of ice cream. S'mores Ice Cream Sandwiches? You've Been Dumped Ice Cream? Family Drama Bananarama "Nice" Cream?

But for today? The day the bomb is dropped? Bad News Berries Sherbet will get the job done. It's sweet to drown out the bitter. It's light to remove some of the heaviness you're feeling. And it's way easy, so you can spend your energy coming up with a plan for what to do next.

CAR CRASH

MINT-CONDITION CANDY ICE CREAM

We wanted to name this ice cream "Crashed Your New Car before You'd Even Made the First Pay Mint." But the name was too long and the experience that gave birth to the name was too painful to share. Let's just say cars were crashed. Tears were shed. Insurance rates were increased.

If you've just crashed your car, regardless of who was at fault, you could benefit from a little ice cream therapy.

Today, enjoy an ice cream that's always in mint condition.

Prep time: 15 minutes
Chill and process time: 2-3 hours
Makes 1 ½ quarts

INGREDIENTS

1 cup whole milk
¾ cup superfine sugar
Pinch of salt
2 cups heavy whipping cream
1 tablespoon pep-
permint extract
½ teaspoon vanilla
12 peppermint candy canes, crushed

DIRECTIONS

1. In a standing mixer, combine whole milk and sugar. Mix until sugar dissolves.

2. Add salt, heavy whipping cream, peppermint extract, and vanilla. Mix well.

3. Process in ice cream maker according to manufacturer's directions. After about 10 minutes, stop machine and add crushed peppermint candy canes. Finish processing.

4. Serve immediately for soft serve, or cover and freeze for 2-3 hours before serving.

5. For an extra delicious twist, top with our Homemade "Magic Shell" (page 119) and a mini candy cane.

GLOOP 2.0

There's nothing like an honest to goodness sick day to send you from zero to doom in nothing flat. When your head aches and your body aches, it's easy to see the world through doom-colored glasses. Food doesn't taste as good. Everything seems louder.

You need a box of tissues, a cup of tea, and a butler to serve you while you lie around thinking dark thoughts. *Pride and Prejudice* may come into the picture. And you have to eat something, but nothing sounds good.

When Kathryn got sick when she was little, her mom used to mix Jell-O and ice cream into a concoction she appetizingly called "Gloop." It was almost worth getting sick just to get the opportunity to slurp this stuff down. Today we prescribe for you Gloop 2.0, a delicious mix of cream and Jell-O and sugar and love.

Of course, it will taste 98.6 percent better if you can get someone else to make it for you.

Prep time: 5 minutes
Chill and process time: 2-3 hours
Makes 1 ½ quarts

INGREDIENTS

2 cups heavy whipping cream
2 cups whole milk
¾ cup sugar
2 teaspoons vanilla
1 package (3 ounces) Jell-O, any flavor

DIRECTIONS

1. Combine all ingredients in a bowl with a mixer or whisk until combined.
2. Cover and chill 2-3 hours or overnight.
3. Pour cold mixture into ice cream maker and process according to manufacturer's directions.
4. Serve immediately for soft serve, or cover and freeze for 2-3 hours before serving.

BAD DAY
Nº. 30

Running On EMPTY

BADA-BING, BADA-BONBONS

Certain battery-operated bunnies just keep going. And going. And going. But we weren't made that way. Thanks, Mom! Instead, we have bodies that fuel up by eating nutritious food, getting adequate rest and exercise, and being exposed to the sun. But we don't always get those things. Thanks, Twinkies and kids and laziness and the Pacific Northwest!

In a perfect world, we would live on broccoli and sunshine. But sometimes we need a little artificial boost to get us through an entire day. For some of you, this involves a cup of coffee. Kathryn's partial to Vanilla Coke.

A burst of sugar also does the trick—the colder, the better. Let these tasty Bada-Bing, Bada-Bonbons bring you back to full power.

Prep time: 10 minutes
Chill time: 1 hour
Makes approximately 15 bonbons

INGREDIENTS

1 pint ice cream
   (Cookies and
   cream, pepper-
   mint, or coffee
   work well, or use
   your favorite)

1 batch
   Homemade
   "Magic Shell"
   (page 119)

DIRECTIONS

① Line a baking sheet or shallow rectangular dish with parchment paper and chill until ready to assemble bonbons.

② Use a melon baller to scoop ice cream balls onto prepared pan and freeze until firm, about 1 hour.

③ Place melted "Magic Shell" in a squirt bottle.

④ Remove ice cream balls from freezer and coat each with "Magic Shell" (which will harden immediately), then return to the lined pan.

⑤ Freeze until ready to use.

BAD DAY
Nº. 31

CARESIVER BURNOUT

S'MORES ICE CREAM SANDWICHES

We all need someone to take care of us sometimes. But some of us need to be cared for all of the time. And for the ones doing the caring day after day, night after night, the burnout is *real*.

Whether you have a newborn who constantly needs to be held and rocked, or a puppy who desperately needs training before he consumes every shoe in your house, it can feel like you're burning the candle at both ends.

Before your fire goes out completely, why don't you roast a marshmallow and turn your burnout into s'mores?

On a day when you need a little care yourself, find someone to take over for you, take a break, and celebrate your down time with a S'mores Ice Cream Sandwich. When you're done, maybe you'll be ready to go back for s'more.

Prep time: 10 minutes
Freeze time: 4-5 hours
Makes 8-10 sandwiches

INGREDIENTS

- 3 cups heavy whipping cream
- 1 can (14 ounces) sweetened condensed milk
- 3 cups crushed graham crackers, divided
- 1 ½ cups chopped Hershey's chocolate candy bars, divided
- 1 ½ cups mini marshmallows, divided
- Additional graham cracker squares to make sandwiches

DIRECTIONS

① In a large bowl, whip cream until stiff peaks form, about 5 minutes.

② Fold in sweetened condensed milk, 1 cup crushed graham crackers, ¾ cup chopped chocolate candy bars, and ¾ cup mini marshmallows.

③ Transfer mixture to a dish or loaf pan. Garnish with remaining graham crackers, chocolate, and mini marshmallows.

④ Cover and freeze until firm, 4-5 hours, or overnight.

⑤ To serve, allow ice cream to soften 5 minutes and scoop onto a graham cracker, topping with another graham cracker to make a sandwich.

BAD DAY №. 32

TORNADOES AND HURRICANES AND HAILSTORMS, OH MY!

STORMY SODA SHOP MALTED MILKSHAKE

Prep time: 5 minutes
Freeze time: 10 minutes
Makes 1 milkshake

INGREDIENTS

1 cup milk
6 tablespoons
  malted milk
  powder
1 pint ice cream
  (chocolate,
strawberry, or
  vanilla)
2-3 malted milk
  balls, crushed

DIRECTIONS

① Process milk and malted milk powder in a blender.

② Add ice cream one scoop at a time and process until smooth and creamy.

③ Pour into a tall glass and freeze for 10 minutes. Garnish with crushed malted milk balls and serve.

*Y*ou wouldn't mind if soccer got rained out today. But if it got rained *on*? If it started pouring and you *still* had to sit on the sidelines for an hour, shivering? Yuck.

And that's just minor weather. What about when a hailstorm devours your garden? Or a hurricane sits off the coast, waiting to strike?

You're not evacuated, but you know it will be a big storm. Gather batteries, water, food—all the essentials—turn on the Weather Channel and wait. As you wait, you might start to think, *I wish I were waiting in an old-timey soda shop.*

I think we've all been there.

The soda shop is probably closed. But, if you have a few key ingredients on tap, you can create the experience right there in your windowless shelter room. Follow this recipe for a Stormy Soda Shop Malted Milkshake flavor extravaganza.

BAD DAY №. 33

DUMPED

YOU'VE BEEN DUMPED ICE CREAM

W e dump things we don't want any-more. Trash. Half-eaten chili dogs. Cute girls whose only flaw was loving a jerkface too much!

You've been dumped. And it feels terrible. If you didn't see it coming, you feel blindsided. If you saw it coming and stayed around for the ax to drop, you feel demoralized.

You're not going to binge eat or drown your sorrows. That path is for lesser mortals. No, you will construct a carefully crafted thematic dessert to cleanse your life of that spaz-nard and celebrate your newfound freedom.

He thinks he got the best of you through an unceremonious dumping? Not hardly. You will turn being dumped into a chocolatey, delicious master-piece. Today is the first day of the rest of your life. Cheers!

Prep time: 10 minutes
Makes 1 serving

INGREDIENTS

1 pint ice cream, any flavor
Assorted cookies, candies, choc-olates, mints, toffee, pretzels, marshmallows, fruits, nuts, sprinkles— whatever your heart desires
Chocolate, straw-berry, caramel, or marshmallow sauce, pur-chased (or make our Optimistic Marshmallow Sauce, page 117)

DIRECTIONS

① Remove ice cream from freezer and allow to soften about 10 minutes. Scoop into a bowl.

② Break any add-ins into bite-sized pieces as needed, and add as many and as much as you desire into soft-ened ice cream.

③ Dig in ASAP or cover bowl and freeze until it's scoopable, about 1 hour.

④ Garnish with sauce and anything else you want!

GiRLS' NiGHT iCE CREAM SANDWiCH CAKE

She hugged you when your cat died and laughed with you when your attempt at French cooking went terribly wrong. Your kids have grown up together and you've always expected to grow old on each other's front porches. Until yesterday.

Your best friend told you she's moving to Idaho. *Idaho!* Who does that? You go together like Mario and Luigi, like beaches and sand, like cookies and ice cream. And you don't know what you'll do without her.

It's time for a little bribery. Wrangle up all the ice cream sandwiches in your possession—an edible parable for perfect friendship—and mold them into a luscious cake she surely won't have access to in the potato state. Then host a girls' night.

On the off chance she still plans to abandon ship, use this cake to lure her back for a visit as often as possible. Best friends can handle a few hundred miles of separation if there's proper incentive to reunite.

Prep time: 15 minutes
Freeze time: at least 30 minutes
Makes 10-12 servings

INGREDIENTS

24 purchased ice cream sandwiches
1 tub (12 ounces) frozen whipped topping
Purchased or homemade chocolate and caramel sauces (try our recipes on pages 121 and 117)
Assorted sprinkles

DIRECTIONS

① Remove ice cream sandwiches from freezer 5 minutes before assembling to allow to soften slightly. Layer 12 ice cream sandwiches in the bottom of a 9×13-inch dish.

② Spread half of the whipped topping over the ice cream sandwiches. Drizzle with chocolate and caramel sauces.

③ Top with another layer of 12 ice cream sandwiches. Spread remaining whipped topping over the ice cream sandwiches. Top with additional chocolate and caramel sauces and garnish with sprinkles.

④ Return to freezer and chill 30 minutes or until ready to serve.

BAD DAY
№ 35

FAMILY

DRAMA

FAMILY DRAMA BANANARAMA "NiCE" CREAM

No matter how great your family is (and we're sure they're just about the best ever), there will be some drama. It's that thing where humans come together in a group and try to get along. It's not always smooth.

Add to that the pervasive feeling that families should agree, get along, be tight knit, and fall in line, and you *know* there will be trouble, because each member of the family is likely still a human person with thoughts, feelings, and desires.

And one of those desires is to belong and be loved and understood. So feelings are close to the surface, and when Uncle Ned makes an unkind comment, pretty soon you're crying into your pumpkin pie and storming from the Thanksgiving table.

When things go bananas at your house, reach for the kind of bananas that are down to earth, healthful, and still as sweet as pie. And because we know that family drama comes in all varieties, this recipe is fully customizable.

Prep time: 5 minutes
Makes 2-3 servings

INGREDIENTS

2-3 ripe bananas, peeled, sliced, and frozen. (Keep sliced bananas in the freezer (in a zip close plastic bag) on the "ready" for smoothies and banana bread, as well as this recipe.)

½ teaspoon vanilla

Pinch of salt

DIRECTIONS

① Blend frozen bananas, vanilla, and salt in blender until creamy.

② Once the mixture reaches soft-serve texture, you can eat it immediately or scoop it into a container and freeze for a firmer texture.

Try these variations:

ⓐ **Chocolate Banana Ice Cream:** Add 3 tablespoons cocoa powder.

ⓑ **Nut Butter:** Add 2-3 tablespoons nut butter.

ⓒ **Berry Good:** Add 1 cup frozen berries of choice.

CHAPTER FOUR

ALL IS LØST

There are days of mild irritation, moderate trauma, and all kinds of worst days ever. And then there are days when you're completely rattled and filled with big questions. Not only do you feel lost on these days, but sometimes you feel like *all* is lost.

A day like this might happen when you feel caught in the middle between two people you love. It may feel like all is lost when you need to make a major life decision or when you get to the end of your rope and feel like there are no good options left. Often these days go on for a long time, because it can take a while to find your way.

So maybe cook through this whole section if you're feeling lost or discouraged, one treat a week to motivate you to keep sending out flares. You will find your way back! We believe in you!

91

CAUGHT IN THE MIDDLE

BAD DAY
NO. 36

BERRY FROYO ICE CREAM SANDWICHES

On the one hand, a giant fort made of milk jugs sounds amazingly fun. On the other hand, you can see how being able to access one's bed and closet sounds appealing. Your two sons stand in front of you, hands on their hips, waiting for you to make a decision on the fate of their bedroom.

It's not fun to be caught in the middle. How can you encourage Bart's sense of fun and creativity and still support Fredrich's need for functionality? You're in a pickle. A jam. A sandwich.

We don't really know how to help you out of this particular swagglebog, but we do know how you can reward yourself after you get it all sorted out: put something else in the middle. We suggest Berry FroYo Ice Cream Sandwiches.

Prep time: 5 minutes
Chill and process time: 2-3 hours
Makes 12 sandwiches

INGREDIENTS

2 ½ cups fresh berries (thawed and drained if using frozen)
1 cup superfine sugar
1 teaspoon lemon zest
2 cups plain Greek yogurt
24 cookies (2-3 inches), any flavor

DIRECTIONS

① In a blender, combine berries, superfine sugar, and lemon zest. Blend until smooth.

② Whisk in yogurt and pour into ice cream maker. Process according to manufacturer's directions.

③ Cover and freeze for 2-3 hours.

④ Scoop about ¼ cup of Berry FroYo on the flat side of 12 cookies, then top with remaining cookies.

⑤ Cover and freeze ice cream sandwiches until ready to serve.

BAD DAY
№. 37

TRUST
NO ONE

OVER-THE-TOP YOGURT POPS

Every dystopian novel has a point where someone tells the main character, "Forget everything you thought you knew about the world. Everything they've ever told you is a lie."

The creepy caste system is actually repressing everyone. The benevolent dictators are murderous fascists. Your parents are robots.

The protagonist stumbles away, reeling, no longer knowing which of the boys in her love triangle is safe to make out with. It's a bad day. A super bad day.

We've had days like that, where our whole world was flipped upside down and it felt like the sky was crashing in.

For a day this mind-bending and insane, you need a crazy good remedy. Throw all the fruits and yogurts and sweeteners in a blender and watch them crash in on themselves, chaos blended together until something smooth and creamy emerges. Then put it on ice (like your cryogenically frozen biological parents) and enjoy.

Prep time: 5 minutes
Freeze time: 4-6 hours
Makes 6 pops

INGREDIENTS

2 cups raspberries, cherries, sliced strawberries, chopped peaches, blackberries, or blueberries

2 tablespoons agave or honey, to taste

2 cups vanilla Greek yogurt

Popsicle molds

DIRECTIONS

① Blend fruit in a food processor or blender on high speed until pureed.

② Pour into a large bowl and stir in sweetener of choice. Add the yogurt and mix well. Add more sweetener if needed.

③ Pour mixture evenly into Popsicle molds, then freeze 4-6 hours or overnight.

FORK IN THE ROAD

BAD DAY

Nº. 38

WHAT'S NEXT NUTELLA

You've been zipping along in your life on a safe and predictable path when all of a sudden, the road splits in front of you. Do you go left? Right seems pretty okay. How about up? Maybe you could just fly for a while.

Maybe you're thrilled to choose a new career or excited to figure out how to spend your time when all your kids leave for college. But it also feels a little like jumping off a cliff. The safety net is gone; you're making this up as you go.

It's so overwhelming! You want to choose the best possible option, the one true path of perfect happiness forever and ever until you come to the next fork in the road. You may feel like you're going nuts.

But going nuts doesn't have to be a bad thing. Sometimes nuts grow up to be Nutella. And then you make them into ice cream and spend some time savoring it while you decide which road to try next.

Prep time: 10 minutes
Chill and process time: 2-3 hours
Makes approximately 1 quart

INGREDIENTS

⅓ cup Nutella
¼ cup superfine sugar
1 ⅓ cup heavy whipping cream
1 teaspoon vanilla
Pinch of salt
Optional: ½ teaspoon espresso powder

DIRECTIONS

① In a blender or food processor, blend Nutella, sugar, cream, vanilla, salt, and espresso powder (if using) until smooth.

② Pour cold mixture into ice cream maker and process according to manufacturer's directions.

③ Serve immediately for soft serve, or cover and freeze for 2-3 hours before serving.

ADRIFT

IN THE WORLD

LOST LEMON ICE CREAM

*I*f you get lost on a hike, Cub Scout wisdom tells you to stop where you are and call for help. You'll be much easier to find if you're not running around the woods looking for your friends.

But what if no one's looking for you? You'd better do your best to figure out where you need to go and head toward civilization before it gets dark or you run out of fig bars.

When you're feeling lost in your life, you may get stuck, waiting to be found. You may wait a long time, and it's cold out there on the side of the mountain—alone.

Cold isn't a bad thing if it's in the form of this Lost Lemon Ice Cream. While you're planning your exit strategy from the land of the lost, mix up a batch of this and restore your zest for life.

Prep time: 15 minutes
Chill and process time: 2-3 hours
Makes 1 quart

INGREDIENTS

1 tablespoon lemon zest

½ cup lemon juice, fresh

1 cup sugar

3 large eggs

2 cups half and half, divided in 1 cup and 1 cup

½ teaspoon vanilla

DIRECTIONS

① In a saucepan, whisk together zest, lemon juice, sugar, eggs, 1 cup of half and half, and vanilla. Cook over moderately high heat, whisking constantly, until it just comes to a simmer.

② Strain the custard through a fine sieve into a bowl.

③ Chill in covered container 2-3 hours or up to 1 day.

④ Whisk in the remaining 1 cup half and half and process in ice cream maker according to the manufacturer's directions.

⑤ Serve immediately for soft serve, or cover and freeze for 2-3 hours before serving.

BAD DAY
№.40

SHOULDA
COULDA
WOULDA

UNICORN ICE CREAM

You can't change the past any more than you can find a unicorn at the state fair. Pigs? Yes. Deep-fried pickles? Definitely. But unicorns are hard to come by.

If you spend the entire day looking for a magical single-horned beast, you'll miss out on all the other glories the fair has to offer: Incredible cleaning products that might possibly still work once you get them home. Roller coasters made out of rust and PVC pipe. Cabbages the size of minivans. You don't want to miss all that.

And you don't want to miss out on all the joy and beauty and possibility of your life because you're stuck in a rut of shoulda, coulda, woulda.

You definitely shoulda. Well, you didn't, and you can't change that now.

If you'd had the tools, you coulda. Well, you didn't have them.

If you'd only known, you woulda. Well, you didn't know.

The closest you can get to changing the past is formulating the future in a better way. *That* is real. That is possible.

Spoiler alert: Unicorns are not. As a symbol of letting go, treat yourself to a little Unicorn Ice Cream. It's silly, it's fabulous, and it's the first step to a brighter future.

Prep time: 30 minutes
Freeze time: 2-3 hours
Makes 6-8 servings

INGREDIENTS

- 3 cups heavy whipping cream, whipped
- 1 can (14 ounces) sweetened condensed milk
- 1 teaspoon vanilla
- ¼ teaspoon cotton candy flavoring*
- Pink, purple, green, blue, and yellow food colorings, gel, or paste
- ¼ cup rainbow sprinkles, plus extra for garnish
- Purchased cotton candy

*LorAnn makes a delicious cotton candy flavoring that can be purchased on Amazon.

DIRECTIONS

① In a large bowl, stir whipped cream, sweetened condensed milk, vanilla, and cotton candy flavoring until totally combined. Divide evenly between five smaller bowls.

② To each of the five bowls, add a different food coloring and stir until color is incorporated.

③ Layer dollops of different colored ice cream base in a 9×5-inch loaf pan.

④ Smooth the top and run a knife through the mixture 3-4 times to swirl the colors. Don't overmix.

⑤ Top with sprinkles and freeze until firm, 2-3 hours.

⑥ Serve with more sprinkles and a small handful of cotton candy.

OUT OF OPTIONS

BAD DAY
№.41

THE BANANAS FOSTER OPTION

There's always a way out, another option. If this job doesn't pan out, you can apply for a different one. If your kids hate PB&J in their lunch boxes, you can offer them cheese and crackers. Options are comforting, which is why it can be so frustrating when they run out.

The comforting truth, although you may not believe it in the moment, is that there are always options. They may not be your favorite, you may need help to uncover them, but there are always options.

One night at a restaurant, Kathryn had a hankering for dessert and there wasn't much to choose from. *There are no options*, she thought. *Bananas Foster? What even is that?*

So she ordered it. And her sweet tooth has never been the same. Today, sample a dessert that proves that sometimes a lack of options can lead you to something new and amazing.

Prep time: 10 minutes
Freeze time: 1 hour
Makes 4-5 servings

INGREDIENTS

1 pint vanilla ice cream
2-3 tablespoons butter
½ cup brown sugar
1 teaspoon vanilla
¼ teaspoon ground cinnamon
3 bananas, peeled and halved crosswise then lengthwise

DIRECTIONS

1. Scoop ice cream into shallow bowls and place in freezer until ready to use. (This step prevents the ice cream from melting immediately on contact with the sauce.)

2. In a large skillet, heat butter and sugar over medium-low heat. Cook, stirring occasionally, until smooth and bubbly, 4-6 minutes.

3. Add bananas and cook, gently swirling skillet, until bananas are just warmed through, 1-2 minutes. Remove from heat.

4. Add vanilla and cinnamon and gently stir into cooked bananas.

5. Remove ice cream from freezer, top with bananas and sauce. Serve immediately.

LETTING EVERYONE DOWN

BAD DAY
№. 42

TiRA-ME-SU SORRY CAKE

You need to attend your daughter's soccer match, but the meeting went over and you can't leave. Keep your job and continue feeding your family or walk out on your boss and make it to soccer on time?

Sometimes you have to make hard choices and you disappoint people.

We suggest a "treat"ment solution that's shareable. You can console yourself about your misdeeds while concocting a tasty peace offering to numb the pain of your innocent victim.

I hurt your feelings when I forgot to pick you up after school? That's fair. I still love you, please forgive me, and look—ice cream!

Prep time: 30 minutes
Freeze time: 2-3 hours
Makes 1 cake (8-10 servings)

INGREDIENTS

2 tablespoons sugar
⅓ cup espresso, hot and freshly brewed
1 family size (16 ounces) purchased pound cake, cut in half horizontally
¼ cup instant espresso powder, divided into 2 tablespoons and 2 tablespoons
2 quarts coffee ice cream, slightly softened, divided
Chocolate sprinkles

DIRECTIONS

① Stir sugar into hot espresso until dissolved and set aside to cool.

② Place one layer of sliced pound cake in a 9-inch square baking dish and brush with half the espresso syrup. Sift 2 tablespoons espresso powder over top.

③ Put 1 quart ice cream into bowl of an electric mixer. Mix on low speed with paddle attachment until softened; spread over bottom cake layer. Top with second pound cake layer; brush with the syrup. Chill in freezer while prepping the second quart of ice cream.

④ Mix the second quart of ice cream in the bowl of an electric mixer until softened and spread over the top cake layer. Sift remaining 2 tablespoons ground espresso over cake. Cover and freeze 2-3 hours prior to serving. Frozen tiramisu can be wrapped in plastic and stored in the freezer up to 3 days.

⑤ To serve, slice and garnish with chocolate sprinkles.

BAD DAY
Nº. 43

ROUGH TIMES AHEAD

ROCKY ROAD ICE CREAM

The road less traveled is less traveled for a reason. It's lumpy and hard and treacherous. But sometimes you see a difficult road stretching out in front of you and you know you have to travel it anyway.

If you just found out you have carpal tunnel and will need months of rehabilitation to get your pickle ball serve back up to par, this ice cream might be for you. You could take the easy route and forget your love of the sport, letting your partner—nay, *humanity*—down. Or you could set off on the rocky road to rehabilitation.

If you choose the rocky road, I suggest you make our Rocky Road Ice Cream to assist in your healing journey.

Prep time: 10 minutes
Chill and process time: 2-3 hours
Makes 1 ½ quarts

INGREDIENTS

2 cups 2% milk
2 cups heavy whipping cream
1 cup superfine sugar
¼ teaspoon salt
1 teaspoon vanilla
½ cup unsweetened cocoa powder
2 cups miniature marshmallows
¾ cup almonds, toasted and sliced

DIRECTIONS

1. Whisk milk, whipping cream, sugar, salt, and vanilla together in a large bowl until completely blended.
2. Slowly whisk in cocoa powder and stir until incorporated.
3. Fold in marshmallows and almonds.
4. Process in ice cream maker according to manufacturer's directions.
5. Serve immediately for soft serve, or cover and freeze for 2-3 hours before serving.

CHAPTER FIVE

THE FREAKIN' CHERRY ON TOP

Once you've chosen the perfect ice cream treat to soften the edges of your bad day, you still have to decide how you'll handle the blues. This section of toppings offers you options for how to deal with your bad day.

So, if you're feeling adrift in the world but you're ready to look on the bright side, make a batch of Lost Lemon Ice Cream and top it with Optimistic Marshmallow Sauce. If you need to wallow for a bit, drizzle on some Hot Fudge Feels. No matter what you choose, these toppings are sure to enhance your "treat"ment!

MOVE On

BAD DAY COPING MECHANISM Nº. 1

Prep time: 15 minutes
Makes about 1 ½ cups

SHAKE-IT-OFF STRAWBERRY SAUCE

INGREDIENTS

1 pint fresh strawberries, chopped; reserve ⅓ cup

⅓ cup granulated sugar

1 teaspoon fresh lemon juice

Tiny pinch of salt

1 teaspoon vanilla

DIRECTIONS

① Heat all but ⅓ cup reserved strawberries, sugar, lemon juice, and a tiny pinch of salt in a saucepan over medium-high heat.

② Bring the mixture to a boil and cook, stirring occasionally, 5-10 minutes, or until the sauce thickens.

③ Remove from the heat and stir in the reserved strawberries and vanilla.

④ Allow the sauce to cool to room temperature before using.

⑤ May be stored in a covered container in the refrigerator.

Are you ready to move on? Whether you're sad, angry, or hurt, sometimes the best thing to do is follow T-Swizzle's lead and "shake it off."

You can literally shake it off with some rad dance moves in your kitchen, or possibly the answer is some positive self-talk, like a fighter going into the ring. "That was rough, but you've got this, Kathryn. Come on. Shake it off!"

If you're ready for a fresh start, move on with our Shake-It-Off Strawberry Sauce. Fresh, fruity, sweet, and sunny. Sauce your way to victory.

BAD DAY COPING MECHANISM

№. 2

WALLOW

HOT FUDGE FEELS

Sometimes you don't want to be cheered—you just want to experience the exquisite pain of your terrible day. If you're not ready to move on from all the feels weighing you down, it may be best to just wallow in your misery.

Put on the saddest movie you can find—one that always makes you cry. Or, if you're really committed, paint on some black eyeliner, write some sad poetry, and embrace your inner emo.

There is no better topping for wallowing than gooey, sticky hot fudge. Let the Hot Fudge Feels drench your food in delectable darkness while you savor the sadness.

Prep time: 15 minutes
Makes about 1 ½ cups

INGREDIENTS

1 ½ cups sugar
1 cup cocoa powder
1 cup heavy whipping cream or half and half
½ cup butter
2 teaspoons vanilla
Pinch of salt

DIRECTIONS

① In a medium saucepan, combine sugar, cocoa, and cream or half and half, stirring with a whisk until completely combined and smooth.

② Turn heat to medium, stirring occasionally as you bring to boil for a few minutes to thicken slightly.

③ Remove from heat and stir in butter, vanilla, and salt. Mix well.

④ Cool for 5 minutes before using.

⑤ Store in a covered container in the refrigerator.

⑥ Microwave at 30-second intervals to rewarm sauce to serve.

LET THE TEARS FLOW

BAD DAY COPING MECHANISM №. 3

CRY-IT-OUT CARAMEL SAUCE

Are your eyes leaking? That's okay! We all need a good cry sometimes. If you're losing water from your eye holes, it may be time to find an understanding shoulder to moisten and simply give in to the flood.

Our Cry-It-Out Caramel Sauce is a tiny bit salty, like your tears, and a little bit sweet, like the relief you'll feel after you let it all out.

Prep time: 10 minutes
Makes about 1 cup

INGREDIENTS

1 cup brown sugar, packed	4 tablespoons butter
½ cup half and half	Pinch of salt
	1 tablespoon vanilla

DIRECTIONS

① Mix brown sugar, half and half, butter, and salt in a saucepan over medium-low heat. Whisk gently for 5-7 minutes, until it thickens.

② Add vanilla and cook another minute to thicken further.

③ Turn off the heat, cool slightly, and pour the sauce into a jar. Refrigerate until cold.

BAD DAY COPING MECHANISM №. 4

LOOK ON THE BRIGHT SIDE

OPTIMISTIC MARSHMALLOW SAUCE

Sure, you burned the stir-fry. But on the bright side, you got to go out for delicious tacos. Someone drove a car through your front window, but at least now you'll get a good breeze blowing through the house.

Some days are rough, but if you look at them the right way, you can see the good.

If you're ready to look on the bright side of your bad day and count your blessings, you're ready to lighten up your mood. Complement this coping technique with the lightest and fluffiest of ice cream toppings, our Optimistic Marshmallow Sauce.

Prep time: 10 minutes
Makes 1 cup

INGREDIENTS

¾ cup granulated sugar
1 tablespoon corn syrup
2 ½ tablespoons butter
¼ cup whole milk
Pinch of salt
½ package (16 ounces) marshmallows, chopped
2 tablespoons water
1 teaspoon vanilla

DIRECTIONS

① In a saucepan, heat sugar, corn syrup, butter, milk, and salt over low heat and stir until sugar is dissolved. Bring to a boil, then simmer 5 minutes.

② In the top of a double boiler, melt marshmallows with the water.

③ Stir melted marshmallows into sugar syrup, mixing completely. Remove from heat and stir in vanilla.

④ Store covered in refrigerator.

BAD DAY COPING MECHANISM №. 5

TOUGHEN UP

HOMEMADE "MAGIC SHELL"

Have you ever seen a toddler who's so mad he refuses to eat? But then he's also hungry, which makes him madder still? Have you ever been that toddler?

It's okay to feel hurt or sad or angry. However, when those feelings are no longer serving you well, it's time to move on. Sometimes the answer is to toughen up a little. If your feelings are continually hurt, maybe you need to develop a thicker skin. If little things keep making you mad, maybe you need to find a way to cope without resorting to anger.

When you're ready to toughen up, make our Homemade "Magic Shell," a delightful outer layer for all the sweetness you plan to create.

Prep time: 5 minutes
Makes about 1 cup
Note: You can make as little or as much as you want. Simply use 1 part coconut oil to 3 parts chocolate.

INGREDIENTS

½ cup coconut oil
1 ½ cups milk chocolate chips
½ teaspoon vanilla
Dash of sea salt

DIRECTIONS

① In a medium saucepan, melt the coconut oil over very low heat. Slowly stir in the chocolate chips until completely melted and blended.

② Remove from heat and add vanilla and sea salt.

③ Cover and store in the refrigerator or at room temperature. If solidified, microwave in 15-second intervals to liquefy before using.

BAD DAY COPING MECHANISM № 6

SWEET SERVICE

EAT YOUR ICE CREAM SPOON

Bad days can turn even the most loving person into a ball of self-centered angst. *Life isn't fair*, we think. *Isn't this just my luck?* We focus inward on our own needs and preferences, and sometimes all that focus turns our sadness into self-obsession.

Often, the best remedy for the blues is to forget ourselves and serve someone else. The Eat Your Ice Cream Spoon is a good reminder that sometimes serving is its own sweet reward.

Prep time: 10 minutes
Dough chill time: 3-5 hours
Bake time: 10 minutes
Makes 12 spoons

INGREDIENTS

- 2 cups all purpose flour, sifted, plus more for surface
- ½ teaspoon baking powder
- ¼ teaspoon salt
- ¼ cup rainbow sprinkles (optional)
- 1 stick butter, unsalted and softened
- 1 cup granulated sugar
- 1 large egg
- 1 teaspoon vanilla
- ½ teaspoon almond or lemon extract

DIRECTIONS

1. Whisk together flour, baking powder, salt, and rainbow sprinkles.

2. Cream butter and sugar until pale and fluffy. Mix in egg, vanilla, and almond or lemon extract. Gradually add flour mixture and mix until dough comes together.

3. Shape dough into two disks; wrap each in plastic and refrigerate at least 3 hours and up to 2 days.

4. Preheat oven to 325 degrees. Roll out one disk of dough at a time to just less than an inch thick on a lightly floured surface. Using a paring knife, cut out spoon shapes about 3-4 inches long, or use a spoon-shaped cookie cutter.

5. Transfer to baking sheets. Chill in freezer for 15 minutes.

6. Bake until cookies are golden around the edges, 10-12 minutes.

7. Transfer cookies to wire racks to cool.

SEEK ADVICE

COOKIE CUPS

Prep time: 10 minutes
Dough chill time: 2-3 hours
Bake time: 20 minutes
Makes 6 bowls

W hether you caused your bad day or you're just really suffering due to someone else's actions, the best person to dig you out is you. But you can't always find solutions on your own. Sometimes it takes the advice of a good friend to give you perspective.

If you're ready to handle the fallout from your bad day with the help of a trusted friend or guru, get one of these cookie cups ready to catch all the advice that falls your way.

INGREDIENTS

2 sticks butter, softened
¾ cup powdered sugar, sifted
1 teaspoon vanilla
2 cups all purpose flour, sifted, plus more for surface
½ teaspoon salt

DIRECTIONS

① Beat together butter, sugar, and vanilla in a mixer. Reduce speed to low and beat in flour and salt until combined.

② Shape dough into a disk and wrap in plastic wrap. Refrigerate 2-3 hours or overnight.

③ Roll out dough to ¼ inch thickness on a lightly floured surface and cut out six 4 inch circles.

④ Place rounds on an overturned 12-cup muffin pan, leaving empty cups in between.

⑤ Gently press over the top of each muffin cup and down the sides, then refrigerate 30 minutes to 1 hour.

⑥ Preheat oven to 300 degrees. Remove muffin tin from refrigerator and bake in preheated oven until golden brown, about 20 minutes. Place muffin pan on wire rack and allow to cool.

⑦ Gently lift each cookie cup from the muffin pan and store, covered, until ready to use.

conclusion

Hopefully our sweet suggestions have helped balance out some of your worst days. But you might be left wondering, "What if things are going great? Will I get to eat a scoop of Nuts-for-Pistachio Ice Cream again?" The answer is YES! You can still enjoy all of these treats on your best days, and every kind of day in between.

Because our remedies are versatile and non-prescription, feel free to enjoy them whenever you get the urge. They are (mostly) non–habit forming and can only make your life sweeter and more delicious.

We wish you luck coping with the bad days, but we truly believe you'll have more good days than bad.

ACKNOWLEDGMENTS

FROM KATHRYN

I want to thank my sweet family—Dan, Claire, Ivy, and Oscar—and my parents and siblings for throwing out great suggestions for this book. Thanks also to KayLynn Flanders, Heather Clark, Janelle Youngstrom, and Noelle McBride for looking at drafts and giving invaluable feedback. And, of course, I couldn't have done this project without the marvelous Barbara Beery and the entire team at Familius.

FROM BARBARA

A big "thank-you" to my husband, who has lived through the writing of twenty cookbooks that turned our home kitchen into an ongoing test kitchen for twenty-five years. Kudos to the genius of Kathryn Thompson for creating the "Best Bad Days" ever, and to my dear friends and cookbook aficionados at Familius.

ABOUT THE AUTHORS

KATHRYN THOMPSON

Kathryn Thompson is a freelance writer and blogger living outside Seattle with her computer-genius husband and three frequently delightful children. She believes that the world would be a drastically better place if everyone understood how awesome they were.

Kathryn is a self-certified, eminently renowned ice cream clinician, with years of experience consuming and prescribing frozen desserts. She has been featured everywhere from the *Today Show* to *The Seattle Times*, and you can find her writing scattered around the internet. Check out her personal site: DropsofAwesome.com.

BARBARA BEERY

Barbara Beery, founder of Foodie Kids Culinary Center in Austin, TX (one of the country's first kids-only culinary schools), has taught thousands of children over the past thirty years through year-round classes, cooking birthday parties, and summer cooking camps.

Beery is the author of eighteen children's cookbooks, including three bestselling cookbooks which have sold over 500,000 copies! Barbara worked as a spokesperson for such national companies as Sun-Maid, Uncle Ben's, Borden's, Kellogg's Rice Krispies, and Step2.

Since 2002, Barbara has been a contributing writer to *FamilyFun*, the country's leading family magazine. She has appeared twice on the *Today Show*, on CBN with Pat Robertson, and her business has been featured in the *New York Times* and *Entrepreneur* magazine, as well as dozens of other local and national publications.

ABOUT FAMILIUS

Familius is a book publisher dedicated to helping families be happy. We believe that the family is the fundamental unit of society and that happy families are the foundation of a happy life. The greatest work anyone will ever do will be within the walls of his or her own home. And we don't mean vacuuming! We recognize that every family looks different and passionately believe in helping all families find greater joy, whatever their situation. To that end, we publish beautiful books that help families live our 9 Habits of Happy Family Life:

- Love Together
- Play Together
- Learn Together
- Work Together
- Talk Together
- Heal Together
- Read Together
- Eat Together
- Laugh Together

Website: www.familius.com
Facebook: www.facebook.com/paterfamilius
Twitter: @familiustalk, @paterfamilius1
Pinterest: www.pinterest.com/familius

The most important work you ever do will be within the walls of your own home.